DREAMS INTERPRETATIONS AND CHRISTIAN DREAM SYMBOLS

DREAMS INTERPRETATIONS GUIDELINES

CHRISTIAN DREAMS SYMBOLS

BRENDA MCDONALD

Dreams Interpretations Christian Dream Symbols
Copyright © 2011 by Brenda McDonald
Distributed by prophetic-ministry.com
No part of this book may be reproduced or transmitted in any form or by any means without written permission from the author.

ISBN-978-1456560584

Unless otherwise indicated, Bible quotations are taken from Amplified Bible. Copyright © 1987 by the Zondervan Corporation and The Lockman Foundation.

Contents

Perceiving God's Voice
Why Teach Dream Interpretation
Do Dreams Belong to the New Covenant?

God Speaks To Us in a Very Personal Manner.
The Common "Golden Thread," is Love.

The Holy Spirit Is the Spirit of Truth.
Dependence is Freedom.

Who is This God Who Knows Me?
Knock, Knock, Knock...I must come in!
Honor God.
Are all my dreams from God?

Why Dream? Why Care About Dreams?
Are "Old" Dreams Still Viable?
Grace, Grace, Grace!
Who Dreams?

Types of Dreams
Let's Interpret Our Dreams.
Record Your Dream As Soon As Possible.
Become more interactive in your Dream.

Hindrances to Dreaming God's Dreams
Can What We Consume Affect Our Dreams?
Emotions and Activities Can Affect Your Dreams.
So How Does Interpretation Come?
Remembering Dreams
When do dreams come to pass?
Basic Interpretation Skills
Symbols and Meanings

Dedication

I dedicate this book to the Wondrous **Holy Spirit**, who so loves me and offers the gift of getting to know God so much more intimately.

I give you all my praise and thankfulness because I know, without your marvelous guidance and love; I would be floundering about in uncertainty.

I love your diversity and the way you speak to each of us, in the ways we may understand you. All this, so we may know God more intimately.

I, so want to know you more! Keep speaking your mysteries to me. Continue to give me insight into what you may be saying.

In all your immenseness and creative power, you choose to dwell in me.

That alone, **you alone**, hold me in awesome reverence of You, my Lord. You are all sufficient!

Dreams and Visions, Guidelines for Interpretation

"For God does speak-now one way, now another- **_though man may not perceive it._** *In a dream, in a vision of the night, when deep sleep falls on men as they slumber in their beds, he may speak in their ears and terrify them with warnings, to turn man from wrongdoing and keep them from pride, to preserve his soul from the pit, his life from perishing from the sword." (Job 33:14-16, 29*

Perceiving God's Voice

How relevant this verse in Job is to us, as people of God. This is a world full of information readily available. The Television, the Internet and through all the amazing informational books available to us, what could hold us back from perceiving God? Most of the time, God will not speak to our brain, but to our spirit.

Libraries and archives of ancient history are available on the internet. Virtually everything we could want to understand is written for us to see. We are indulgers of information, on all levels and that helps us relate to the world around us.

Yet in this verse, God warns us about not perceiving Him when He speaks. ...*"man may not perceive it."* We may so often dismiss a dream, because we do not perceive it as God's voice. His messages do not come to us the way a man writes or talks. **I always thought God just spoke English.**

What was I thinking? How did I suppose anyone that didn't speak English understood God?

God speaks in the form of the parable, story, example and the symbol. A dream is the perfect canvas for communication from God.

I truly believe that God is so multi-faceted and multi-dimensional, that He is entirely beyond our human comprehension. He is conveying His purposes in more ways than we could possibly understand. He is so gracious to speak into our human limitations by using our spirits, our inner voice, to translate to us. I am so grateful to God that He conveys messages in human understanding, so we can begin to "hear" what he is saying. I believe one of those ways is dreams.

"God will send us messages in our dreams to help correct, protect and certainly guide us. "

Learning to perceive His voice, and then understand what He is saying, will become more and more crucial, as the days move forward.
It is wise to remember, anything heard or perceived in any way that does not reflect

or bear witness to the character of God, must be disregarded as not of God.

We have been made aware, and now see the evidence, as the "Light" becomes lighter the "Dark" will become darker. To me, this manifestation seems to reflect itself in the distorted messages that are being received by the unsaved. In their quest for truth, they are bombarded with second heaven, demonic or dark spiritual messages.
The "psychics" and "new age" are hungry for spiritual information also. This is a **"golden opportunity"** for the Children of God to come forth with Jesus, the real "Truth."

"One godly interpreted dream will change a life."

The Holy Spirit inspired interpretation, could save a lost soul that is in the bondage of deception. The lost of this world have a **grim need**. The need to know **Jesus is aware of them and loves them.**

"It took one dream, and one interpretation and Joseph sat at court."

Let's hunger for His Words! Let's spend more time understanding God, instead of all the other information available to us combined. God is infinitely more interesting and valuable to us. God's revelations bring us to a place of peace and certainty.

Join me in this quest to understand, "The Dreams We Dream".

Why Teach Dream Interpretation?

This teaching is to help restore the understanding and knowledge of God to the individual and the corporate church. *..."let us know Him and be zealous to know Him."*
(Hosea 6; 2-3)

To take Jesus to the streets for the great harvest of Souls.

One third of the Bible is about this type of communication with God. We need a working knowledge of **the way God speaks to us,** even when we are asleep. **We need to stretch our comfort zone** by going after all God has for us.
Joshua told the people "when you see the Ark go after it. It is the Living presence of God." Joshua also told them to have courage, *"because they had not passed this way before."*

We can say this daily when we attempt to walk in the spirit. Nothing will seem to make sense to the natural mind. It is because we have not passed this way before. God's ways are not our ways, nor are His thoughts are thoughts.

> "It's about expanding your horizons in God. Truly, "His ways are not our ways, and His thoughts are not our thoughts."

If you feel comfortable staying in your logical left brain, you may have a bit of a stretch to move over your logical thinking and try to use the creative right side of your brain.

God created both sides of our brain to be used in accord. Neither can be disregarded. We need the left logical side to read and understand the Word of God, and the right inspired brain, to receive the revelation and the Rhema word. The living, breathing word that is intertwined within the Logos word. After all is said and done **"the Living breathing Word"** is where we receive our sustenance.

There is more to just having dreams and trying to understand and interpret them. We must earnestly seek God to speak to us and give us understanding. We must ask, seek and knock. Ask God for more dreams, let the last words of Thankfulness on your lips as you drift off to sleep, be in grateful expectation of increased revelation through dreams from God.

We must increase our faith for dreaming, by reading about God's prophets and their dreams. Become familiar with the Bibles symbols, and increase your symbolic vocabulary.

Learn to become more perceptive in your dreams, or become more lucid as you dream. This takes a conscience effort to know that it is possible for you to become more interactive in your dreams. I find this to be very helpful if I need a question answered about the dream. When we start to look around in the dream, we may be able to ask a question of an angel in the dream.

You need to learn to think symbolically. This will take some study and practice. Increase your vocabulary of symbols. The more your understanding and vocabulary of symbols increases, the more prepared you will be to think this way as you endeavor your interpretation.

Keep in mind, and we will explore this later, that a symbol may mean something different to different individuals. As you start your journey, look into scriptures for the meaning of symbols. Biblical symbols are more universal and understood by believers everywhere.

Dreams, as we start to look into the Biblical examples, are one of the many ways God talks to people like you and me. **This form of communication is just one of the infinite ways the Lord speaks to His hungry people.**

For instance, Jacob received his greatest blessing from God through a dream. The ladder was given in his dream as the example of an "Open Heaven" available to him. (Gen.28:12).

Joseph was given a prelude to his future in a dream many years before it came fully to pass. Some maturity was needed here in revealing it to his brothers, but all in God's perfect plan, and timing. (Gen.37:5)

Pharaoh also received a night vision that showed him coming events concerning Egypt. Daniels night visions were tremendous. These examples are well worth studying, to see the symbolism of God. (Dan. (7:1)

Do Dreams Belong to the New Covenant?

Some may try to argue against dreams by saying that dreams were God's way of speaking to people under the "Old Covenant."

Listen, as Peter speaks under the "New Covenant." This is right after the Tongues of Fire descended on them at Pentecost, and they were filled with the Holy Spirit.

"And it shall come to pass in the last days, God declares, that I shall pour out my Spirit upon all mankind, and your sons and daughters shall prophesy and your young men shall see visions and your old men shall dream dreams." Acts 2:17

Also, just a note about this scripture, **he was not saying dreams are just for old men**, but this was Peter quoting a type of psalm called Hebrew parallelism. This type of psalm is a song that repeats itself in different words. This type of psalm attempts to paint the larger picture by including sons and daughters, young and old, dreams and visions.

So, as we can see, no **one is left out of this promise**. God says He will pour out His Spirit **on all Flesh**. This is the Gentile and the Jew. This is the saved and unsaved. This is the Christian, Protestant, Catholic, Muslim, Hindu, Buddhist, man, woman, child, young and old. All mankind!

"We will have more and more opportunity's to reveal Jesus to the unsaved by interpreting their dreams. Let them experience, how God alone, is the answer in a dark and troubling world."

My goals in writing this piece are to help you increase prophetically under **the Spirit of Wisdom and Understanding.**

1. To help you to utilize a Biblical dream dictionary and the Bible concordance in interpretation of your dreams.

2. To start to know your own individual symbols that are relevant to you so you may begin to interpret the dreams, visions and prophetic words you receive from the Lord.

3. And last but not least, to receive a higher level of interpretation that goes beyond symbols and directions and comes straight from the very heart of the Father.

Remember this beloved:

"Things are hidden temporarily only as a means to revelation...for there is nothing hidden except to be revealed, nor is anything (temporarily) kept secret except in order that it may be known." (Mark 4:22)

God Speaks To Us in a Very Personal Manner

If you are someone like me, you may have had many dreams over the course of your life. Perhaps you have become more interested in your dreams now, and realize **they may play a significant role in direction and guidance** from the Lord.

I truly trust with all my heart, as we seek the Lord in these matters of supernatural encounters, whether it is His dreams, His parables in the night, or in our waking experiences with Him, He will show us "His way," to receive godly inspiration and direction from the Holy Spirit.

I remember as a small child, I always seemed to have such **striking dreams.** I would wake up my sister and "share." I think she thought her little sister was losing it totally, or she wore earplugs. I remember the strange looks she gave me, but that didn't stop me, I was determined to share my adventures. She just happened to be sleeping in the same bed.

These dreams of mine, I so dearly loved and gratefully escaped to, when life seemed overpowering. Little did I realize what the Lord was showing me.

I believe the Lord showed up in His most gracious way as the counselor, teacher, comforter and friend, to keep me uplifted in times of difficulty.

I remember when we were young; my father would get laid off from his job in a machine shop.
Until my father was working again, we relied on help from Social Services.

Mom would take us all to the welfare office for some of the powdered milk and eggs and some other food-like items that I can remember seeing, but can't remember now what they all were. I think that is because they were indistinguishable from real food. Yummy.

I just wasn't able to eat those powdered food-stuffs. I became quite thin during those few times, we needed the provisions.

> "During those tough times, I would have the most wonderful dreams with Jesus."

We would be sitting in Heaven, at the longest, most sumptuous banquet table I had ever imagined. In fact, there was no end to it, and it seemed as wide as the horizon.

As I recall, the table was in a room of a large opulent castle, with fireplaces made of massive golden rocks. The fires, in these enormous fireplaces, would always be burning brightly and the handsome room was cozy and warm.

I remember the walls were filled with amazing paintings. There were scenes of different people doing great feats of courage.

I remember thinking, "Oh! That looks like Moses." or "Oh! That looks like Abraham."

> "I was dazzled by a painting of the most beautiful bride, I could ever imagine!"

She was painted in the most joyful colors. Her dress was luminously white. It appeared bejeweled with faceted diamonds. The diamonds reflected the "Light" and the room up sparkled with a rainbow of color.

"I thought the Bride was alive!" It looked to me as if she would move in the painting ever so slightly. When she did I felt my spirit leap.
As she moved, her dress shown like a rainbow of colors. "Oh!" She was so brilliant, that I had to partially close my eyes to look upon her. She appeared like the brightest sunny day. The more time I spent in Heaven; the more my eyes were opened to her beauty. I remember saying to myself, *"I will look like her someday!"* How glorious she appeared to me.

I watched Jesus closely and noticed He was particularly fond of the painting named simply, "The Bride." He looked at her longingly.

"I could tell she was someone very exceptional to Him, and I wanted to be just like the bride."

On the banquet table, was every imaginable food and goodie in amazing abundance. I recall the smell of the room. It was so wonderfully rich and intense, filled with exotic aromas. Even the smell that the bounty of food produced made me feel at home. I was overcome with the sense of Love and being nurtured so completely. All the cares of the world never entered my thoughts.

There were fruits, and cakes, bowls of gorgeous food, large platters of unusual and colorful things to eat. Most of the food was as lovely as was tasty. I really couldn't recognize most of it as being earthly food. I do remember the donuts in particular, they were soft and sweet. It all tasted very good.
There were no powdered eggs in Heaven ....glory to God! There really is a banquet table.

There were sweet animals with us also, gentle dogs, kittens, lions, elephants and many others. They talked to me and played all around Jesus and I. The animals were more beautiful than any one of its kind here on earth. I've always loved

God's animal kingdom, so this was a special treat just for me.

Jesus and I would just sit there all night and eat together. Not too much was ever said between us, just mostly a lot of smiling! I mean, it is hard to speak when you are stuffing your face with doughnuts. It was glorious!

I looked around at the palace and enjoyed the beauty of it all. I believe this experience has molded my taste in household decorating. I still am drawn to traditional tapestries and ornate frames and rich deep colors. I dress in these colors and fabrics too. Until now, I hadn't realized this about myself. See how writing the vision down brings more revelation and an increased understanding of the full impact being with Jesus can bring.

I would wake up feeling quite satisfied, and joyous at the bounty of food, I had available to me. I could hardly wait to go back to see Him again.
Mom always wondered why I was going to bed so early. I wished I could bring some of those great donuts back to my

family. No "doggie bags" in Heaven I guess. Everyone needs to get that heavenly nourishment on their own.

This could be a great movie, I think.

Well, perhaps when you were younger, you had many dreams as well. At some point these dreams may come back to you. Take note as you recall your youthful dreams. It's wonderful to see what Jesus did for us all through our life. He never left us, even when we weren't aware of His faithfulness to nourish us.

Seek the Holy Spirit for a recollection of these clues into your development. You may be pleasantly surprised as to how **the Lord guided and protected you through your formative years.** These are the real meat of your spiritual development. This is supernatural development of your character.

As we grow older, our life experiences, and our circle of family and friends expands. Our joyous moments and trials become more complex and unique.

Our brain and spirit become full of an ever mounting array of knowledge from a multitude of sources. Our personality, our persona, **our character, is forming from our life experiences both natural and spiritual.**

Our minds and spirits are like receiving antenna, ever ready to take in that which surrounds us. All that information is interpreted, by us, in our own frame of reference. So, what means something to you may make no logical sense to me, and vice versa.

God in all His uniqueness and diversity has made us in His image. No two of us are the same.

"Our emotional and spiritual components and the uniqueness of our personality, all contribute to the way we hear God."

The Common "Golden Thread," is Love

The exact situation in both of our lives will yield to each of us our own personal set of thoughts, and ideas wrapped around it.
Again, I perceive differently than everyone else. You perceive differently than everyone else.

"We are as individual in thought and perception as God has permitted us to become."

And yet in all our multiplicity, in God's creativity to make us so, He has allowed us to relate to each other in a **common golden thread, which is Love**. Love for each other will draw us closer. Love will cover a multitude of sins, our own and others. We must learn acceptance of our individuality, and a genuine appreciation of each other's peculiarities.

Ultimately, we realize if we criticize or judge one another, we are criticizing God's creation. We are "one body" so in fact, we are criticizing our self, as well as God. The Love walk is a walk in loving yourself also.
God has created you so entirely unique, that no one will ever been able to do what you were called to do. And, no one that is ever created again will be able to do what you are called to do.
You were truly beautifully and wonderfully made for "such a time as this." We know each and every one of us is God's beautiful creation. See yourself as God sees you. See others as God sees them. We are perfect while being perfected, God's perfect creation.

    "After all, it's God's diversity that we see in each other. Look a little deeper and you will see God in His glory."

This is what will weave the "Body of Christ" together. His Glory and Love woven into a garment without spot or wrinkle. His promised one, "The Bride." The beautiful painting that I saw in my dream as a little girl.

"She will finally come to life. Not just the hint of movement that I saw, but a fully living, breathing "Bride."

The Holy Spirit Is the Spirit of Truth.

"Ultimately, absolutely and utterly, all interpretation must come from the Holy Spirit.
Having said that, I believe we are the best interpreters of our own dreams and visions **through the unction of the Holy Spirit.**
In the greatest humility, and in appreciation of each other's gifts, we will receive much help from each other. Through others experiences with God, we may see a different perspective of the same experience. The Holy Spirit will bear witness in our spirit, and we will know the interpretation.

God created us to be in relationship with Him and each other. We are given gifts to do the good works.
Therefore, we will never see the whole picture without a little help from our brothers and sisters in Christ. God will give each of us that little puzzle piece, to help one another, see a larger picture, a more complete picture, of the revelation.

Dependence is Freedom

God is so perfect in His plan! **Dependency** on God for all aspects of this interpretation process is His eternal plan. Thank God we are not left up to our own devices when trying to understand these spiritual principals.

This makes me feel a whole lot of freedom in this process of interpretation and teaching. Trusting the Holy Spirit to take hold of the reigns and steer me in His direction.

With Him to rein me in and keep hold of me tightly, **I have freedom to explore His**

way. I only have that freedom, because of my utter dependency on God. I love being dependent and under the guardianship of my Lord and My savior, Jesus Christ.

So now what? Well, as you start to get the bigger picture, we can understand that God will use our "frame of reference." God will use Biblical illustrations, parables and examples, to speak to us in a dream or vision. This is the language and vocabulary of the Spirit.
The "***language of the Spirit***" which is the parable, and our very own symbolic frame of reference, will go into a very personal message from God. ***God truly is in to speaking*** very "heart to heart" and "spirit to spirit" with us. This all boils down to; this dream is really about what you will recognize, at a given place in your life, when you take the time to look into it.
So now we understand as we develop a little more, and our life experiences amplify, we become more complex. We meet more and more people, we travel, we receive ministry, our consciousness is increasing, the observations and "memory bank" input is also increasing.

We receive some healing in our inner man and we mature.

Our knowledge and understanding of the "Word," enlarge. We read God's word and **assimilate** it into our spirit. We add more complexity and "paint" to our life's palette.

With this palette, God can paint even more **multifaceted dreams**. You see as we mature God may use more symbolism because our depth of understanding is maturing also.

When we first start looking at our dreams they will be pretty simple and literal. If they are literal, interpret them literally. An example may be, you are in your natural car, going to your real job, and a dog jumps in front of your car you swerve to miss the dog, and end up in the ditch. I may interpret that as a warning dream and be attentive on your way to work.

However, let's look at a similar dream that is a bit more metaphorical. You are traveling down an unknown road, in a vehicle that you are unfamiliar with, the car is blue, but you wonder why you are in it. A big black dog jumps into your path and you swerve to miss it and end up in the ditch. This may be interpreted as, you are on your life's road, and you are traveling along, not just standing still in life. Something is coming your way (a faith building experience, (the- dog symbol) that will throw you off for a while, (the ditch) but you will have the revelation from heaven (blue car) to get going on the right path again. In this dream **you** were in the blue car, so I believe it will be **you** yourself that will get the revelation (blue).

I guarantee you that if you were in a room of 50 people and asked for an interpretation of this dream you may get as many interpretations.

 Probably you know already of a possible event that is coming your way, and this will speak very personally to you. This dream gives you some options too. Having had this dream before a particular life altering decision will arm you with the knowledge of some possible consequences.

The difficulty in these interpretations is you still can make choices. Your dreams may give you a warning, but if you choose to ignore it, well that is our free will. If you become "frozen with introspection,"

pray about it, and seek the help of your pastor. Hopefully he will have the Holy Spirits insight for you and some godly wisdom thrown in. The Holy Spirit will always lead you into Truth.
Pretty soon, you will start to understand your dreams and will truly look forward to this form of direction. It is a learning process, and will develop more and more. As you are faithful in the little things, God will start to give you dreams for your church body, city, state and nation. Even dreams about people you don't know yet, but will.

"Everything we take in through our five senses will influence us, when it comes to our dream experience."

So I highly recommend guarding your "GATES" so to speak. Remember, everything, the good, the bad and the ugly, becomes part of your memory bank. You may very well end up dreaming part of that movie you just watched.
Of course, all that certainly depends on how spiritually sensitive you are. I know individuals who can watch anything on

television or see any movie and seemingly be unaffected. Where this is concerned for myself, if see violence or otherwise non-edifying behavior in movies or TV, I will most certainly see it again as it replays itself in my dreams.

*Some of the dreams we dream could be just a **natural result** of the many levels of subconscious we have.*

In other words, as a natural process, we may have fragments of the people, places and things stored within our minds that are floating around, at just below conscious level. These are experiences of the soul, ideas and desires, so to speak. These dreams that are related to our natural experiences and come as a mass of fragments that make no sense are quite normal. Certainly these are necessary to "defragment" our wonderful computer brain and dump the junk we don't need.

Do you have a hard time trying to figure out if the dream you had was from God?

This may be easier than you understand it to be.

I find if certain **particular characteristics** are involved in and around the dream, I am relatively certain it was from the Lord.

Some of these particulars are characteristic of a dream from God; if scripture is spoken to me or written somewhere in the dream, if I awaken suddenly and know God has spoken to me, if I am reminded of the dream again and again throughout my day, and if I feel the need to pray after I wake. Oh, and if the dream stays with me forever, I find this very important.

Sometimes the dream is very vividly portrayed to me with a concise message and I bear witness to the character of God in the message.

If I am speaking with someone and the dream is brought to my remembrance, to edify or comfort someone. Dreaming with Jesus is His testimony too.

Who is this God who knows me and brings these dreams?

Let me give you a little story to show you how this "personal" God might fit this all together.

I recently invited a dear artist friend to visit with me for the weekend. After much fun and laughter and lots of good eats, we decided to paint a still life painting together. I totally enjoyed watching her grab fruits and vegetables, vases and lovely fabric in her arms and lug the whole bunch of it upstairs to my loft area. She lovingly arranged the whole lot just so wonderfully. When the subject was ready, away we went on our painting adventure.

Several hours had passed and we were totally enjoying this moment of creativity. So immersed in our own interpretation of what we were seeing and recreating with paint, that we didn't notice what each other was indeed reproducing.

Finally, I took a peek at her rendition of the still life we both painted, and *was stunned! How different our two paintings appeared.*

How could two people seeing and experiencing the same objects, at the same time, using the same mediums of oil paint and canvas, produced such a different interpretation of what we saw? She was more theoretically correct and her hand more practiced than mine. Her rendition was more realistic and colorful. Her paints had not been mixed too much to "muddy them." She saw the colors in a different way than me. Even the shapes of the objects were done as her eye saw them.

Her painting reflected her experience, maturity, and love of brilliant and electrifying color to enhance the mood of the painting. *Her "eye" and experience had influenced her interpretation*

I painted the vase, vegetables and background in more subdued colors. My objects were done in a softer palette. The mood of my whole painting was a quieter and more placid version. I liked the tranquility of seeing the fruits and vegetables and vase and cloth like a banquet. I felt serene as I looked at the finished canvas.

These interpretations were both acceptable, and both recognizable as the objects to be painted. Then with the touch

of individuality, a separate interpretation immerged. How marvelous!
God has created us as individuals and He alone knows who we are and how to paint us. God alone knows how we see the world around us. When He speaks to us, He knows what color palette to use. God alone knows what tiny little nuances that we can relate to, in the language we understand. Yes, and He is faithful to do just that. He will speak to us in our dreams in pictures we will understand.

"He truly is a personal Savior, full of Love and grace."

Knock, Knock, Knock...I must come in!

So it all begins, because we seek, we ask, we knock! See the hungry of heart. See the thirsty soul seeking a drink of cool refreshment from the "Living Waters". Our gracious Holy Spirit will begin to illustrate to us the revelation of **how key our dreams are**.

By using the concepts we have accumulated in our own spirit and mind, He will use "*our palette*" to help us investigate and begin to **recognize what God is saying to us.**
Interesting enough I see this truth in this scripture:
"**However the spiritual is not first, but the natural then the spiritual."
I Cor; 15-16.**

Are you willing to seek Him? Are you willing to know Him in a more intimate way? Do you truly desire to take this road to enrichment in hearing Him speak in your dreams? This journey is one of intimate **exchange** and fellowship with Him who redeemed us?
The apostle Paul said this;
"**God will use the foolish things of the world to confound the wise."(1 Cor. 1:27)**
If our dreams seem foolish or senseless to us at first, do not disregard them. This is truly a learning curve.
This is an enrichment process that will change your spiritual life forever. Understanding the dreams you dream will add a new dimension in the spirit.

"This will be the "Jack hammer" in your spiritual toolbox. "
This tool will open up your eyes and ears to a gift waiting to be given to you by God.

Honor God

Paying attention to our dreams is **honoring** God by listening to Him in the way He wishes to speak to us at that moment. This is "Waiting upon Him."

"But those who wait on the Lord shall renew their strength: they shall mount up with wings like eagles, they shall run and not weary, they shall walk and not faint".
(Isaiah 40:31)

"Dear Holy Spirit, I humbly submit these thoughts and conclusions I have realized, as a result of my personal experience with You. My prayer is that through the inspiration of my dearest counselor and comforter, the **Awesome Holy Spirit**, I may facilitate someone in their search for a deeper reality of God. Thank you, Holy Spirit, With Love in Christ Jesus."

Are all my dreams from God?

"And without faith it is impossible to please Him for he who comes to God must believe that He is, and that He is a rewarder of those who seek Him." (Hebrews 11:6)

If someone were to ask me if my dreams were all from God, I would have to say no, but, I believe that many of them are. I also know where the "*real* "of God is, the enemy will always come in to counterfeit. As a matter of fact, we as perceptive and sensitive people, are susceptible to dreams from a multitude of strange and dark spirits that would like to keep us in a state of fear, or just out of the resting place of God. These are readily recognized by their character. The Holy Spirit will teach you how to deal with these types of dreams.

"The key to distinguishing the origin of the dream is by the character of the author."

Undoubtedly we know **the character of God**. He is everything good, pure, holy, full of light, color, joy, immense love, majesty, loving kindness and eternal Life. This is a very inadequate list of His characteristics. It would take an eternity of pages, to describe how marvelous He is. Then certainly, paper would come to its end.

Oh, the other author? That would be beelzebub, author of lies. Characteristics would be death, no life, no light, no love, and no edification, no color, nothing good. Got it? Of course we know who has come to steal, kill and destroy.

So what would that dream be like? Yep, you got it. No life, no light, no love. Dream scenes that are scary, and hateful, dark and full of condemnation, to name a few of these his distinct traits.

Hmmmm, seems pretty easy to distinguish, doesn't it? Careful here though, the fallen one does come in many disguises. Trust the Holy Spirit to guide you. *"Lean not unto your own understanding."*

We are the children of "The Light," we will have the help of the Holy Spirit. We will discuss this later again, because this particular point does seem to have some in bondage over their dreams....who can they trust? Our awesome God! He will keep us covered under His wings. So trust our splendid God for direction.

I am so much in *awe* of how our most wonderful, merciful Creator, loves us, that I have the faith to believe that **my steps are directed by Him**.   He even governs my sleep time, and uses that time to assist me. I desire My Lord, Jesus Christ, to direct and counsel me in these times of sleep, when my spirit is most vulnerable and open.

Why Dream? Why Care About Dreams?

Praise God forever.
The dreams the Lord has graced me with over the years have always *astounded* me. His dreams have become so precious to me that I am so very thankful for His grace and mercy to direct me this way. Let's go on a journey to see how we can utilize these precious "night Visions." Let's explore some understanding and particulars we will benefit from as we journey with God.

Are "Old" Dreams Still Viable?

Now, often times I have a dream **brought back to my recollection.** Something I once dreamed and had long forgotten. That dream was deep in my spirit ready to bubble up when the time was right. These dreams are still utilizable and when this particular type of dream is recalled, it becomes living again, anointed, and now I see it was set aside for such a time as it was needed.

I believe that these particular dreams are a very life giving and an anointed way the Lord may use to **minister to others.** This is just another example, of how we may minister out of our past memories, prophetically.

For example, I was ministering to a group of believers and the Lord brought back a dream I had as a youth. **A dream I couldn't possibly have understood** at the time I dreamed it. However, it had much meaning, as I stood before this group of earnest believers. God gave them direction on how to proceed in the advancement of God's Kingdom in a way that would help them bypass many pitfalls.

As I stood before them, and as I prayed for "The Word of the Lord" to come forth for them, I started **recalling the dream.** I felt quite strange as this never happened to me before. So I but proceeded to verbalize the dream. This recollection came **so suddenly,** and so particularly, I knew it was the Lord's word for the moment.

This particular dream came to me when I was about eight years old. *Jesus came* on the scene, as a humble carpenter's son. We were in a desert and I saw Him from a distance. He was talking to a very young dark haired girl. They were standing by a **striking oasis of fresh turquoise waters and breezy palms.** His long brown robe was belted at the waist, with an exquisite golden rope.

*"His hair was dark, long and wavy, He was amazingly beautiful, but it was His **radiant and majestic** countenance that was so remarkable."*

His eyes were so very endearing and I could tell this lovely man was full of compassion and love with no condemnation or judgment. **So full of grace!**

I felt so peaceful and wanted to come closer to this "Radiant One." I felt the desire to hold His hand, and no sooner had I thought this, the little girl was gone, and I stood in her place.

Jesus took hold of my right hand and we walked and talked. I asked Him who He was, and He said ,"I am the Lamb of God." I looked at Him again, and knowing I didn't understand, He just smiled. He was **lovely** to me and I was a very much in awe, with my new friend.

I realized in the dream that we were in a "Middle Eastern" market place. There were men and women **selling " healing remedies**." I could smell the extraordinary spices. I heard the many voices and sounds of the busy market place. The men wore turbans, and the women long dresses and colorful, ethnic type clothing.

Jesus, holding my right hand, led us to a particular group of merchants who were attempting to demonstrate their ability to heal.

These men had turbans on their heads and they were chanting strange words and giving glory to some unknown god of theirs.

The woman, who needed healing, appeared to be in severe misery. Nothing seemed to be happening to her, and she remained in her difficulty.

I noticed then the men had completely **disappeared from the scene.** Jesus then looked down at me and smiled and said **"because I love her so much."** That was all He said and then He looked up at her and she was healed.

Later, **years later**, as I contemplated that scene with Jesus, I thought how one look from His compassionate eyes, His *great love, will heal our infirmities.*

Nothing the "Hindu's" could do or say would bring about the true healing from our Savior. No chanting or praying to idols, nothing we can do in our own strength would make any difference. I saw how quickly the men disappeared and only **"The Truth"** remained

Jesus and I walked on to the next group of healing merchants. This was surprising, since they looked like Western business men in business suits. They were asking for large donations into their baskets. They were offering **healing for money**, American Dollars to be exact. All of them had large *Peacock feathers* in their hands. They were waving them over the diseased people, and praying in a very flamboyant manner. The infirmed looked quite vulnerable and continued to give them more money.

Credit cards were being used and repeat charges were being made. The sick were not being helped, but the debt was building in their lives. I saw the **"Proud as a Peacock"** men continuing to collect from the poor. I saw a fire from heaven fall upon these men and burn them, and they were no more.

Quickly the scene changed. I asked Jesus if I could get Him something to eat. We got in my car, and started to drive. Ahead on the road, the traffic was backed up for miles and seemed we would be stopped for hours if not days.

Jesus told me to go around the cars and so I did. I noticed that many of the cars were trying to *push each other to move forward.* This was causing a lot of jealousy and anger if one car got a little ahead of the others.

There was a military tank trying to push one of the little cars to get going. It seemed the tank would roll over the little car, and it would become absorbed into the tank.

Jesus just, shook His head in disappointment, and indicated that I should just go around them. I did and the way was made clear, to drive forward. I knew as long as I had Jesus with me to show me what to do and how to do it, I would be able to press on, and steer my way clear to the banquet table.

The Interpretation came as this;

The little girl in the dream was me, I was just eight at the time of the dream, and the Lord was helping me to understand Him even as a child. In the dream I became a young adult, as I started to grow in understanding and revelation.

We were standing next to the cool pool of Bethesda. I believe that pool represented true healing, by Jesus' sacrifice, through faith.

The palms symbolized a place of Victory. The breeze symbolized the wind of the Spirit, the Holy Spirit.

The "Hindus" in the dream represented the

" **new age**" spiritualists who try to heal by way of formulas and rituals. Formulas and rituals will be used by those in witchcraft. This will quickly pass as the end of the age draws closer.

The second group of people were using peacock feathers. Have you ever heard of the phrase "Proud as a peacock?"

We know that if intentions are wrong, if we are trying to get the glory for the good work, if we touch what is rightfully **God's glory**, we are treading on shaky ground to say the least.

And finally in the dream the Lord had me pass all those cars (that represent individual ministries). It seemed they were stalled on the road. They were trying to push each other out of the way, so they could get ahead. The tank, (a large ministry) was running over the smaller cars (ministries) to try and absorb them or destroy them. ***Possibly they had missed Jesus***, and were independent of Him instead of dependent on Him. It seemed much better to have Jesus in my car, (my ministry), to guide and direct me. I did not want to stay in the stopped traffic of ambition, confusion and greed.

Better to have Jesus in your ministry than being independent of Him. "Oh Lord, please don't give me my way, I tried that and I know my way doesn't work. Please Lord let me know Your Way only."

So you see the power of this one little dream. It helped and instructed me years before it helped and instructed a whole church body. Glory to God!

Grace, Grace, Grace

As I look back on my experiences with the Lord, I am still astounded by the things He has revealed to me. I have had questions answered, comfort, correction, and I have seen things to come in time for intercession. God is so faithful to get what you need in time for when you need it. Dreams are some of the most intriguing times in my life with our Lord. He makes the journey interesting and fun. He has also shown me His most wonderful self. I have met Jesus face to face. His beautiful face has been is etched in my mind forever. In these times with the Lord, my faith has grown. When you look upon Him, all things are made new again. No pain, no trauma, no sin, no condemnation, can dwell near Him. The recesses of your heart can be set free, so He can fill you with His healing Love. So He can inhabit the temple within you. He wants all of you! I want all of Him! These are all **miracles** that you have to look forward to. These testimonies will swell your faith to dream with assurance and see for yourself.

"Faith is the assurance of things hoped for, the conviction of things not seen."
(Hebrews 11:1.)

My faith has been renewed many times in my dreams. Times when I so needed the help of the Lord to keep me joyful, He has been there for me. So, you may now see, how important sharing an understanding of this spiritual tool, this gift, is for me.

Dreams are for now, dreams are for you. Praise God that we are forever on His mind. Praise God that, He so graciously desires to communicate with us, Spirit to spirit.

Dreams are the perfect place for Him, to talk to us. We can't argue, with Him, we just need to observe and ask a few questions.

When we lay our head down to sleep, who better to entrust our spirit to than the Holy Spirit?

Take joy in our Most High God, worthy to be trusted. Dreaming is not for the so called "super-spiritual". It is and always will be for everyone. Seek Him and you will find Him.

Who Dreams?

Everyone dreams. Yes, it is written,
 *"**we shall prophesy, see visions, and dream dreams.**"*
*"**And it shall come to pass in the last days, God declares, that I will pour out of My Spirit upon all mankind, and your sons and your daughters shall prophecy (telling forth the divine counsels) and your young men shall see visions (divinely granted appearances), and your old men shall dream (divinely suggested) dreams." (Acts 2:17).***

We believe that God reveals Himself in prophecy, in visions, and in dreams. We understand and accept this fact because the Scriptures witness to this time and time again. When we receive the Holy Spirit, all believers, as it is written, with no discrimination to gender, or age, will know Our Lord in a supernatural way. These are God's promises and we stand on His word. We will dream dreams. Be bold. Go forth and dream as you never have before. Be assured, that with purity of heart, you can and you will, dream the Lord's guidance, comfort, direction, and yes, warnings and rebuke.

Types of Dreams

Emptying

We all dream. If we did not dream, we would be unable to deal with all the input we have during our life. Some dreams are just a cleansing by the grace of the *Holy Spirit*. This includes nightmares. These dreams will appear a nonsensical mix of scenes, people, places, flashes of light and darkness, mostly indescribable and very forgettable.

We have all had these types of dreams. They can really be very disappointing when you are so hungry for a word from the Lord. However they are inescapable and may happen during seasons of change.

Solutions in dream

Who better to receive our answers from, than our Great Counselor?

If I have a need of an important answer, I seek the Holy Spirit specifically about my concern. I pursue the Lord till I get the answer. I trust Him for the timing of the answer also. Sometimes I receive an answer in a dream, and sometimes I do not.

One particular instance comes to my mind, when I received my answer in the form of a night vision/dream.
I was going through a very difficult time in my life and needed some godly council. I thought about my mother, who had passed several years before that. Mom would always have the right answer at the right time. I so missed her guidance. She would always have the most wisdom, and she was the one I trusted the most.
A few days passed, and I had a wonderful dream about my mother. In the dream, oddly enough she was seated next to her casket and was enjoying a cup of tea. She told me to have a seat. Mom motioned that she was no longer in need of "that" as she pointed to her final earthy resting place. Later, as I thought about what she said I concluded that indeed she was resurrected with Jesus and sitting with Him at the right hand of the Father. Who needs a casket? She asked me what was on my mind and we proceeded to have an in-depth conversation of what was happening in my life. I received the answers that I so desperately needed. I felt peaceful and rested when I awoke.
I believe the Holy Spirit was sitting there with me in my Mothers earthly form.

This will happen from time to time in dreams. The Lord will use a familiar form to give his motherly advice. The symbolism may be obvious or not. I've dreamed of my best friend in high school only to realize that indeed Jesus is my best friend. He used a familiar face to get His point across that He was my best friend.

Intercessory Prayer

Dreams will cause us to pray. Particularly, if in your dream you witness a disaster or impending danger of some type. Perhaps you have had a dream about a friend in an accident or mishap. You can use this dream as a warning, and intercede against the plans of the enemy. Of course you would never want to scare someone by telling them your dream about them, instead you would pray for their safety and protection. You would ask the Lord to send forth angels to protect and watch over them.

Could this dream have been from the enemy? Of course...but how you use this dream is up to you! You could have scared the person you dreamt about by telling them the dream. They may have gotten into fear and caused an accident. Instead you walked in wisdom and love and prayed them through it.

I have an example of this type of intercessory dream from many years ago. In the dream, I saw a young pastor who I did not know. He was killed by the enemy in a severe battle. I saw his face, as he was dying. He looked up to me for help. I was compelled to pray. I remember I was sobbing in my sleep, and began to pray for his restoration. I awoke and was still praying till the sorrow lifted. The victory had been won.

A few weeks after the dream, my husband and I were at a business conference in Atlanta.

On Sunday, after the conference was completed, we attended a church service for the participants. We were seated in the back of the hall and the service was very crowded. We really couldn't see the ministers on the stage, because we were so far back. I felt the unction of the Lord to go up and meet the ministering pastors. When the service was over, I headed the long way to the front of the hall. As I got closer I recognized the man in the front. He was the young pastor in my dream. To say the least I was astonished. I wasn't quite sure at that point what to say or do, but the Lord graciously showed up. I asked the young man if I could pray for him. I prayed renewed courage and faith, and gave him a word that the Lord was holding him up in all his concerns, and the enemy had no hold over him. I prayed no weapon formed against him would prosper, and cancelled the assignment of death off him. God is so good!

The dark Side

At times and in seasons the enemy may invade your restfulness and peace by entering your dream life. When I was quite young, the enemy kept me in constant fear over the death of my mother. He perpetually entered my dreams with fear of losing her, and being left alone in this world. I would go to bed hoping not to dream those dreams. An old friend of my mothers gave me a book full of pictures of Jesus. I would meditate on those lovely pictures before I went to sleep. This helped tremendously and the dreams became less and less.

These types of dreams are from the enemy, and are designed to keep you from freedom in Christ. They keep you living in a perpetual state of exhaustion and depression.

Dreams like these may mean, you need deliverance from a particular spirit, like fear or anxiety. You may need some healing in those places you were traumatized. This was what happened to me when I was young and vulnerable. The spirit of fear and abandonment attached itself to my spirit. Only Jesus can help you in these areas. Seek His Face when you feel troubling come over you. He will be faithful to help you and fill your heart with His love. **Jesus will show you how to heal your heart.**

Recently, in a dream, I had an experience with Jesus in this restorative manner. I had been feeling quite unsettled in my heart. I finally realized I needed to go to my Savior for help. I had a vision of a little girl in a large dark room. She looked really scared and alone. I looked closer and it was me. So, I asked Jesus where He was and a little Jesus doll appeared in my hand.

In the next scene, in the vision, I was in a deep well. I was still very small and fragile. I was desperately clutching to my Jesus doll. I saw a rope fall down into the well and I grabbed hold of it. I was just too little to climb it. I just didn't have the strength. I could have tried with both hands, but then I would have let go of Jesus. Just then, I looked to the top of the well, and had a prophetic vision within this vision. I saw myself sitting at the top of the well in the bright sunlight. I saw the end of the story, but didn't know how to get there.

I was beginning to get angry and frustrated with myself that I was too weak and no one was there to help me. I felt if I didn't get up the rope on my own there would be no one to come to my rescue. After all, I knew everything had to be done in my own strength.

Jesus was about to rock my world. At that moment of deep despair, a very large bucket came down the well next to me. The bucket was full of blue waters and lots of swimming fish. It looked like an ocean in a bucket. I quickly jumped in and began swimming joyfully with the fish. I came up out of the water to see that Jesus was no longer just a doll. Jesus was a very large, bright and shining man. He grabbed hold of the rope, and became the counter weight so I could be hoisted up to the top of the well in my lovely bucket swimming pool. As I watched Him, descending into the dark pit and disappeared. When I got completely to the top, I looked over the edge, and into the darkness, hoping I could see Jesus. He was out of sight. Then, after what seemed like an eternity of waiting, He began to ascend back up the well towards me. As he got closer and closer I saw a set of keys in His hand. He looked glorious to me. Completely out of the dark pit, we sat at the top of the well together. I realized He had gone into to the pit to set me free. He had recovered the Keys to Death. I had watched His resurrection. Needless to say I was astonished and an amazing flood of emotions came over me. He put a lovely blue scarf over my hair and the vision ended.

To Help Others

On a ministry trip to Wales, I recognized that spirit of fear and anxiety; I had as a little girl. When I got this word of knowledge from the Lord, I came near to her, and we talked. She confided that she had been having fearful dreams about her parents leaving her all alone. I broke off the spirit of fear and abandonment and prayed a release of the prophetic spirit that rested in her. I imparted pleasant dreams from the Lord for her, and asked her to give Jesus her heart. Her father later testified to me that she was dreaming more pleasant dreams and was joyful. God is so merciful to each of us. What a blessing for me to know that the Lord turns all things for good, for those that love Him. This little girl had been spared a childhood of nightmares, made my trials worthwhile.

I'll never forget her little sweet face as we said goodbye, she said to me, "I love you and I will never forget you." How much more reward could one ask for?

As children of the Light we can interpret these types of dreams and shed the Light into the darkness and use it as a blessing to help one another.

The enemy will perpetually probe our "old man" for weaknesses that he can use to keep us from peace. This is true in our waking state as well as our dream state.

We are in a state of being perfected, so not all our dreams are of God. Of course as we discussed earlier, there is a very valid way to know if a dream is from God...God's messages reflect His character of love and compassion and grace, and will always line up with His Holy Word.

Instruction
God gave Joseph a dream before Christ was born. It was an angel who appeared to him in a dream to reassure Joseph that Mary's child was of the Holy Spirit. Joseph had been disturbed about Mary's pregnancy and was concerned what to do. The scriptures are full of examples of God's instruction in dreams.
In these dreams from the Lord, it seems that the Lord closes the ears to our soul, or removes the hindrances from hearing him. He speaks spirit to spirit in our dream. Did you ever awaken and the dream seems like you actually lived it?
 In the words of Elihu, "*He seals the instruction*". The dream is unforgettable and it feels real. Dreams like these will stay with us most of the years of are lives. Sometimes the dream will come to pass long after it had been dreamed.

Years ago I had a **repeating, and instructional** dream that I would live in North Carolina. I had this dream several times over the course of several years. I told my sister that someday that is where I would live. I would tell her that Jesus and I drove there in His car, and He showed me where I would live. He told me I would live in the "Blue Mountains". This was a regular visitation from the Lord and we frequently drove around the world and He taught me geography. I was only 6 or 7 years old when I started dreaming this dream about North Carolina.

Having lived in Pennsylvania the first 40 years of my life, I never really planned on moving. I bought my first home and was working as a Registered Nurse in the hometown where I grew up and had all my friends. As my life played out, and as things happened in a most unexpected way, here I am in North Carolina.
My husband and I are living in the "Blue Ridge Mountains." We have a wonderful view of the "Blue Ridge Parkway." Here is where I was born again, and met my most treasured friend and spiritual father, a

seasoned and well respected prophet, Bob Jones. I would say essentially, this is where my gifts and calling came into full bloom. Had I not moved here I would not have had the opportunity to be mentored by one of God's generals.

The repeating dream, of North Carolina, was a dream from God, of a **promise that would come true** in my life. It was only recently I recalled that childhood dream, and "Oh, what a blessing that was!" How good that I dreamed Jesus took me in His car to North Carolina, to begin my ministry with Him, my wonderful Jesus.

Repetitive dreams

Dreams that repeat themselves over and over may well be the Lord trying to get His point across, and it is a very important point.

Joseph said this to Pharaoh:

"**And Joseph said unto Pharaoh, The dream of Pharaoh is one: God has shown Pharaoh what He is about to do, ...And for that the dream was doubled unto Pharaoh twice; it is because the thing is established by God, and God**

will shortly bring it to pass (Genesis 41:25,32).

As we can see from this scripture, Joseph believed that repeating dreams are from God. He also told Pharaoh, it is an established thing from God that will come to pass. You may notice these in your dream life too. Pay close attention. These may also present themselves with a different set of circumstances, but the same theme, same message.

Cautionary!

God will warn you in dreams if you will pay attention. An example of a warning we all remember the story of Pontius Pilate's wife. As Pilate sat upon his throne, his wife sent him a message that took his breath away.

"Also while seated on the judgment bench, his wife sent him a message, saying, Have nothing to do with that just and upright Man, for I have had a painful experience today in a dream because of Him.(Math. 27:19).

Of course when Pilate heard this warning from his wife, he took heed and proposed a release of a prisoner as a political gesture to show Roman mercy. When he

gave the crowd the choice they chose Barnabas.
He probably thought they would have selected Jesus. Now he had to wash his hands to appease his guilt, and release his accountability.
Pilate tried to heed his wife's dream, but failed in his double mindedness. Please the people, or heed the warning. We still have choices in spite of the warnings.
A couple years ago, my husband and I were pondering expanding our business to a second location in Florida. We had a store already in a resort hotel, but the business was very seasonal. We needed somewhere to sell for the winter when the summer tourists were not coming to the hotel. We sought the Lord in prayer but were still unsure. In our own minds we felt we needed to open the second store, but desperately wanted the go-ahead from the Lord.
My husband had a dream and in the dream he was looking in a mirror. He pulled his left eye open and a fly flew out from his eye.
Having been quite taken aback with this dream, he recounted the dream to a friend, who moved in the prophetic. This man said he had a fly in the ointment of

his eye, but now it was gone and he could see clearly. It seemed logical but we had a "check" in our spirit that this was not quite the right interpretation. At this point, we felt we may be on the right track, and we opened the second store in faith. The store failed and it was obvious the Lord was not in it. What we thought was confirmation, was in fact not. In hindsight, we realized the interpretation was incorrect. We knew then what the dream actually meant. In the dream the fly did fly out of his eye, but his vision had been affected by an assignment of the enemy against his vision. Hindsight being 20-20. A subtle misdirection by an incorrect interpretation that was very costly.

We learn, as the Holy Spirit adds line upon line and precept upon precept. Practice in interpretation and knowing God's Word is vital in this process. Another example of a warning and intercessory dream is this.

I had a very odd dream that seems quite amusing, but had a significant impact on me.

Sometimes in my dreams I seem to awaken and sit up and observe the events as they are played out in my bedroom. My

husband is quite use to finding me sitting up in the middle of the night on the edge of the bed observing the night vision.
On this particular night I sat up to observe four kittens sitting on individual chairs with little name tags, on pretty blue scarves, wrapped around their necks. Each kitten had a letter on the scarf. The most unusual thing about them was, they had no heads. Now you would think I would have been unnerved by these headless kittens, but I wasn't. I observed their little scarves, and saw the letters S, P, U, GS. Each kitten represented a letter, and the forth kitten had the GS on his scarf. Well, I just sat there staring at these kittens and finally asked the Lord, what does this mean? He told me that these kittens were representing the church. SPUGS stood for, selfish pride, and ungodliness.
With these characteristics, the church would have no vision. By cutting off their heads, the way they were thinking, control and ungodly ways of pride and selfishness, they would have a fresh vision from the Lord. This was a warning for the "Body" to repent and change her ways from selfishness to Godliness. This

was a warning dream and a dream that caused me to pray in intercession.

Dreams Not of God?

They are barren; they have no purpose in the Lord's work. If they are not from God they are void of life and cannot give life. They will not produce growth or clear direction in your life. It does not contain God's word and returns void. They are caustic in nature. They do not benefit you. They offer no counsel of the Lord. They fill you with negative emotions that will follow you when you wake. They oppose God's Word. This will be obvious to the discerning Christian. It must line up with the Word. They will discourage you. It will provide no comfort to you. It will promote depression and confusion. These often come in times when life is in transition and you are having turmoil in the soul. They will pass as you enter into God's restoring word.

More Ways to Recognize God's Dreams
God's dreams will always lead you to a closer bond with Jesus. They will lead you down the path of righteousness and purity.

<u>The will build up the Body of Christ</u>, by the teaching and revelation by the Holy Spirit.
<u>Also they will outfit you to minister</u> as the Holy Spirit instructs you. Dreams from God will <u>always line up with the Word of God.</u>

      Let the Holy Spirit be your guide. The Lord spoke to Jeremiah;
"if you return(and give up this mistaken tone of distrust and despair), then I will give you again a settled place of quiet and safety, and you will be my minister; and if you separate the precious from the vile, you shall be My mouthpiece.(Jer.15:19)
 Let us learn to separate the precious, those dreams given by God, from the vile, those dreams not from God.

Let's Interpret Our Dreams

The scriptures are filled with dreams and their interpretations. The Bible gives us instructions on how to interpret our dreams.

In the Bible God used symbols to show His dreamers what they needed to know. God is the same yesterday, today and tomorrow. God speaks the same way to us, today in our dreams. Our dreams use symbols just like the Bible. If we know this, interpreting **becomes a study** in how God used symbols in His Holy Word. One of the best tools you can use is a Bible **Concordance**. This book is invaluable to anyone who is willing to search for their answer. This book is also very helpful if you receive a prophetic word from the Lord for someone. Often times, the words I get from the Lord, come in the form of a symbolic picture. I always have to interpret what they mean before I can give them. This gives me time to understand it and go into scripture to see what it all means. With the Concordance, I can find the scripture quickly. Also there are many books with Biblical symbols. Now of course the internet is filled with searches that can help you.

I highly recommend that you stay away from books, or internet sites, that are written for the "New Age" types. I have looked through these and find them quite disturbing and untrue. Most of the symbols in these types of books have a definitive motive toward hedonistic and soulish desires. Vain imaginations, and not for the "Believer and seeker of the "Truth."

I confidently believe that most dreams are **for the dreamer, and about the dreamer**. As was pointed out, they are instructional or comforting etc., to the one who dreams it.

We all have our own" frame of reference" which the Lord uses to help us understand what He is saying to us. Be vigilant when you attempt to interpret someone else's dream, as you may be using your" frame of reference" instead of theirs. Symbols right out of the Bible, will cross over into every believer's dreams. I have found dreams that are more for the corporate Body of Christ, will have strong symbolism and examples that are distinctive to the Bible.

When I am asked to help someone with the interpretation of their dream, I always ask them what the particular elements in the dream mean to them.

I have heard this example of how our differences can be this extreme; If someone in India dreams of a cow it may mean religious bondage to him. If a farmer dreams of a cow it may mean provision to him.

Record Your Dream As Soon As Possible

Writing a dream down as soon as possible is key in the interpretation process. I have been known to get up in the middle of the night to record something I truly felt was from the Lord. This is a true test of desiring to know what the Lord is speaking to you. It takes a lot of effort to get up out of that cozy bed to write. The Lord says in Mark... *"unto you that hear shall be given more."(Mark 4:24).*
 I want to hear more and more, so I am faithful when the Lord is giving me precious insight, I want it all. My husband bought a voice recorder for me. I hardly have to wake up now to record the dream. If you should decide that you want to record the events in your dream, make note also of people, places, climate, winds, colors, time of day or night, the absence or presence of light, your emotions in the dream, direction...north, south, east, west etc. You will record as many details as

you can remember and more will come as you write the dream also.

Details will amaze you later in how they will influence your interpretation. Look around in your dream, get the details! Look at your clock when you wake in the dream. Some times scriptures and numbers with significance will be given in the element of time.

Record these things and break it down to its simplest form and start to build on it from there.

Determining **who the dream is about**, and **what the dream is about,** will make dream interpretation a whole lot easier. If we cannot properly determine these factors, it will be difficult to interpret correctly what the Lord is saying, and who is He saying it to. Ask yourself this question as you start to interpret your dream, who is this dream about, and what is this dream about?

"Sometimes understanding is as simple as noticing if **you are an observer** or are actually **participating in** the dream."

You as the Observer in the Dream

I very recently had a dream of my friend.

In the dream I observed that she was seated in an old car. The car looked like one of those small compact cars from the 1980's. Her purse was open and I saw from a distance that it had a stack of $80 bills in it. I immediately thought, there is no such thing as $80 bills.

I also noticed she had three umbrellas stacked against her side door. The umbrellas were three different colors, blue, green and gold. It was then I realized in the dream that the steering wheel was on the right instead of the left. The way European cars and English cars are made. I also noticed that her car was in a bit of disorder. The papers and books were scattered here and there.

Well, that morning, was our regular time of prayer and intercession. We called each other as usual. I had actually forgotten the dream until something she said, sparked it back to my memory. She mentioned something about needing to clean out her car, and she found an umbrella near her door. At that point in our conversation I recalled the dream. We were both excited as I started telling her about it. In the dream the Lord was showing me some of the past event in her life, I couldn't have known.

She had owned a small compact car in the 80's. She indeed did have an umbrella in her car at the moment. She had recently been to England on a ministry trip. (Left sided steering wheel.) Neither one of us was really getting the $80 bills though, till we started to get some interesting revelation, as we talked. She was born again in the 80's. Psalm 80 had some deep meaning to her life. I felt that she was being rewarded with a financial and spiritual blessing because of her sacrifice to help many of God's people come out of bondage. All the $80 bills represented the currency of heaven, which are souls. This was her true reward. The true treasures were the people she has counseled back to life. I also felt the three umbrellas represented her gifts of revelation, (blue), the priestly teacher, (green), and a carrier of His glory, (gold). The number three represents the Trinity, being in full participation in her ministry. The unkempt car represented her life as being too busy and needed some attention to get out the unneeded trash. In a sense she needed to reorganize her priorities. When we go back over the dream together, the Lord continues to show us what He is saying to her. It is still living and giving life to her. This is a characteristic of a dream from God. It continues to give edifying life and direction.

The Lord had a plan for that day, since we were scheduled to pray anyways, He purposefully gave me the dream the night before. God had given her some clues to spark my memory.

So we see from this dream example, that indeed this dream was not for me, but for her. I was simply a spectator of what was happening.

If you find yourself as an **observer,** probably the dream will be for **someone else,** and not for you. It seems as we draw closer to the Lord our dreams become more frequently for someone else.

You as the Participant in the Dream

Now we also can become the main character in the dream. During these dreams, when you are actively participating in the dream, it's a pretty good chance you are experiencing a dream about **your particular condition** or need. Note this as you journal your dreams, how you participated, who you talked to, what happened around you and how did you feel.

I have a dream to illustrate actively participating.

In this dream I was in a peculiar city, the streets were full of shelves with intricate goodies for sale. Everywhere I looked, people on the streets were having a huge party. It reminded me of what "Mardi Gras" must be like in New Orleans. I felt vastly uncomfortable and out of place. A man came near me and tried to seduce me. I had to run out of his way. My neighbor was in the dream and was enjoying herself, in the midst of this immoral atmosphere. I grabbed her and told her we needed to leave this place as soon as possible.

At first she resisted then looked at me and came away with me. We got to my house and she needed to go home. Her house is actually up the mountain from me. In the dream, she had a bicycle. She looked at me and said "the only way I can find my way home, is through your house, in your elevator..."

I woke up with a start and realized I would need to do some intercession for her and help her find her way home to the heart of Jesus. Her bicycle represents her personal movement with God. You walk with your feet; you move those pedals with your feet. Sometimes we need another's spiritual uplifting (the elevator) in intercession and example to find our way "Home."

This is just a simple example of how when we actively participate in the dream, good chance the Lord is directing us and the dream is indeed about us. In this dream, I would lead my neighbor to salvation. Also, take note, there was more detail, the goodies etc. but the main thing was the main thing. God wanted to tell me my role in her life. We will go back and see the little nuances of the dream, as we look at these details later. The details are important and will also bring revelation. However, don't lose site of the main message.

Friends and Family Network

I often see, friends and family used as symbols. Sometimes my sister is used to represent the church, sometimes she just represents herself. Also people in your dreams may have already passed on to be with the Lord. Use the way you remember them, as clues as to what the Lord may be speaking symbolically. Also, just the fact that they are no longer living," dead" could mean spiritually dead, as in, that church is "spiritually dead", "dead to self", as a few examples.

Once, in a dream of mine, I saw a large stainless steel pressure cooker, like the pressure cooker my mom used at home in Pennsylvania. Only, this pressure cooker was as large as an airplane hangar! I climbed up to the top of it, peered in, and saw a most unusual site. Inside the pressure cooker was what appeared to be many people lying very still, as though they were dead! I looked closely, and I saw my father lying there also. Someone from a distance said," Look they are all dead." I peered in again, and saw some of them were stirring, with a little bit of life. I yelled back to the "voice", "No, they are still alive; all they need is a little water." I began to pour an endless jug of fresh water on them, and sure enough, they rose up and came alive again.

In a week after the dream, I went on my regular visit with my husband, to see Bob Jones. Bob asked me if I had any dreams and I told him this odd dream about the pressure cooker. He quickly knew what this dream was about.

My father is an ardent Catholic. He was in need of the fresh rhema word of the Spirit. ("Watered by the Word,) to bring him back to spiritual life. To be baptized by the Holy Spirit. The water would be the gentle pressure (pressure cooker) he would need to get him "filled". This was so true, and a very good interpretation of this odd dream.

Also, others would be put in my path that would need the Word of the Lord, to revive them. How exciting to me that God had a plan for me, to be instrumental bringing those people into the Body of Christ, by pouring the Word of the Lord on them.

In this dream my father played himself. That of course made the interpretation a lot easier. This was a relatively "simple" dream to interpret. I did not have the skills yet to see it, but Bob helped me understand how to see the symbolism.

When you begin to interpret your dreams, the Lord will keep it simple so you can progress into the deeper things of God, at your own pace.

As a quick note here," Father" could have the meaning of ("heavenly Father"). It did not in this dream, but see how the Lord will substitute symbolic people to help you understand what He is saying.

My husband had a dream from the Lord and when he awoke he told me, "I had a dream about my oldest, dearest, friend." I said, "who is your oldest, dearest, friend?" Well of course, Jesus is, isn't He?   In this dream Kenneth had an awesome visit from Jesus.

Sometimes the dreams may contain people that **will represent you.** These people may be relatives or friends, even strangers, and their words or their actions will represent something about ourselves that may be good or bad. Sometimes God uses this method to reveal something about our character, through another person in the dream. This may include what we are lacking in our character. We may be able to spot the splinter in another, but not the plank in our eye. If these characteristics of ours are too painful, He is merciful to reveal them, through the actions of another. Thank God that in His mercy, He will lead us to righteousness, by revealing to us, our need for change, and repentance.

Becoming more interactive in your Dream

"I saw at night, and behold, a man was riding on a red horse, and he was standing among the myrtle trees which were in the ravine, with red, sorrel, and white horses behind him.
Then I said, "My lord what are these?" And the angel who was speaking with me said to me, "I will show you what these are."(Zechariah 1: 8-9)

This is a good example of interacting with those people present in your dreams. We note through the scriptures that many dreamers interact with those involved in their dreams.

You can do this also. If you are dreaming, and you see someone you are curious about, talk to them. Interact with those in your dreams; ask questions of them as we see Zechariah did frequently in his dreams and visions. Often, you will receive your interpretation right then as you are dreaming. This is also a good way to "test spirits." If they deny Jesus, you can be sure they are not God! I find that once you are truly aware that you are dreaming, you can become involved in a more active way. I trained my brain, by making an effort to recognize and say out loud in my dream, "I am dreaming now."

"Call to me and I will answer you and tell you great and mighty things you do not know."(Jeremiah 33:3.)

Study the Word

I truly believe you must study God's holy Bible, so that the "frame of reference" you acquire is God's reference. Everything that influences you will become part of you. Isn't
"The Word" a wonderful gift that we may keep our influences pure. The more you entrench yourself in the Lord's Bible, the more you will comprehend what the Lord is speaking to you. You will have a greater ability to interpret suitably. The provision of the knowledge in the Bible will set you free. The beginning of wisdom in all you do, including dream interpretation, will begin with your reverential awe of God. Learn to know God through His living Bible stories.

Develop a personal relationship with Our Lord.
Have faith in God, believe and contend for revelation of what and how He is speaking. Earnestly seek spiritual gifts.

"for whoever shall say unto the mountain and believe it unto His will it shall be done."(Mark 11:22-24)

Are there roadblocks to Dreaming God's Dreams?

Are You Skeptical?

I have been told that I believe most of what I know from God by faith. He tells us **"that without faith it is impossible to please God."**

This is so true of me, personally. I really do believe, by faith and the examples of the great characters of Bible stories, that God blesses me with supernatural experience that must be received with childlike faith.

I was dreaming wonderful dreams from the Lord long before I knew Him. And now so much more since I have run after Him for a closer relationship.

Perhaps you are one of those people who have a hard time accepting the incontestable fact that the Lord really still does speak in dreams.

 I would offer you this, <u>be penitent,</u> ask the Lord's forgiveness for not being an open vessel for whom, He can pour fresh oil into. Ask Him to show you in a way, that will turn you completely around, to receive His nighttime insights.

Just think of all the revelation, insight, and comfort, you have denied yourself and others. Don't be hard headed and hard hearted. We need all the help we can get from our Faithful Lord Jesus.

"If the Holy Spirit is willing to do those wonderful things to enlighten us, let's grab on and not let go."

Let us receive all He has for us. Open up your eyes and be a receiver of those precious dreams and visions from the Lord.

Let Us Have Right Intentions

We must have the right intentions for desiring dreams. Why do you really want to dream anyways? The Lord's dreams are given for all the right reasons. Let's get our heart in order before we come before the Lord and petition Him for Godly dreams.

"God won't bless us if we want to use the dreams to appear spiritual, hurt or control someone."

Our motives have got to be in alignment with holiness. If you aren't dreaming the things of God, maybe you should check your heart.

Can What We Consume Affect Our Dreams?

Ever heard of the so called "pizza dream". This joked about concept has a sound physiological basis. Our body being so wonderfully complex is affected by all that we eat with our mouths and all that "we eat with our eyes." If you eat something that is spicy, or perhaps you are allergic to, your entire physical system kicks in and adjusts the chemistry of your body. Or perhaps there is an unusual chemical in the food you just ate, your brain will sense that it is an unusual substance and have to work overtime to correct the chemical balance in our bodies.   I have found that cold medicines and antibiotics will affect the content in my dreams. I try to be aware when I need to use these medicines that this is affecting me in all ways, including my dreaming perception.

Also, I believe that all you observe with your eyes, good and bad, will affect your dreams.

Personally I have never been able to watch violence or horror movies on television. They will come back to haunt me in my dreams.

My brother would watch the "Three Stooges" when we were growing up. I never liked them, because they slapped each other around so carelessly. Even though we all realized it was done in jest, it all seemed so incredibly cruel.

 So, I am sure I am overly sensitive to the unkindness that is so often portrayed in the media, but I protect my spirit at all times.

Protect **your** spirit at all times. Let's nurture our spirit with positive input, not violence and horror movies. You may find it helpful to listen to soft music before bed. Praise music works quite well to sooth the soul and spirit before bed. Reading the Bible is the best of course. I prefer to pray "in the spirit" to relax before sleep. Fill up your own spirit with peaceful, wonderful thoughts and good spiritual food, then you can dream out of the abundance of love and peace in your heart.

Emotions and Activities Can Affect Your Dreams

You will find also that the state of your emotions and your activities during the day will have an impact on your dreams. Take all this into consideration when you attempt to interpret your dreams. Remember all that affects you during the day will affect your dreams at night. Review the day you had previous to the dream. You may find clues as to why you had that dream. If your day has been particularly stressful and your joy is low, take that into consideration, have a lot of grace for yourself! God has a lot of grace for you!

Taking Computer Classes

My husband and I took a computer class, to learn how to build web pages. It was really difficult for me to assimilate all the new information and I had to study rather rigorously. For several days after beginning the classes, my dreams were filled with computers and computer data Web pages and information of that nature. Very annoying stuff actually.
In one of my dreams, the Lord showed me a miniature computer that had come alive. It walked into my bedroom, (get the picture of a computer monitor with feet?) and was holding fresh baked bread on a silver platter.
I was **encouraged to start writing** on my new computer, and I began this mini-book you are reading now. The computer represented my mind figuratively. Of course the bread it was serving was manna, **fresh revelation** and food from God. The silver represents righteousness. It is my prayer that I am accomplishing just that. Glory to God.

If you understand the term **"play on words"**, this can be very important to your interpretation. For instance take the word cold. Cold may mean temperature in the literal meaning. It can be also be used in a figurative manner. To illustrate this you may say, "He is cold." This is to say he needs a blanket or a coat to warm him up. He is physically cold.

Or you might say," He is cold," and be referring to how friendly, or rather how not so friendly he is. Keep this in mind when you are interpreting your dreams. I have found this to be the case as the Lord is speaking to me. The Lord will interchange these meanings so you will dig a little deeper into the interpretation. As I said earlier, we all have our own personal experiences to add to our symbols.

Sometimes the symbol will not be in the Bible and only relate to you. Or it may be in the Bible, but will mean something different to you in different seasons of your life.

For instance I have a pet cat; this kitty is precious to me. Some people think of cats as sneaky and cleaver to get what they want, and independent, so they have no loyalty. You know... come to think of it, they are a lot like that. But they have their good side too. "Oh," yes, and didn't witches use them and keep them around for their purposes. Not to mention superstition and evil spirits.

Well in my dreams, I have had my cat represent something really sweet, and loyal and tender. Also, I have had big black cats represent bad things, unclean spirits, and even death to self.

It is all a matter of trying to keep things in context and knowing who and what the dream is about.

I had a dream, Jesus and I were in the balcony (upper room, place of spiritual things)of a grand theater.(a place where you go to experience the good things, you learn and observe). The Lord was talking to me about wonderful spiritual mysteries and I was so enjoying just looking into His sweet face. Beside me, was this rather large black cat. (My old self, my old nature.) This large and very loud cat kept meowing; I was being distracted from what the Lord was saying. I was thinking in this dream, *"why doesn't the Lord get rid of this cat for me? He must know I can't completely concentrate on what He is saying with this jabbering, meowing, nuisance sitting beside me."*

I looked at the Lord, questioning Him with my eyes. He simply smiled and continued on with His story. The big cat just kept on pestering me.
Finally, I grabbed hold of the cat and threw him over the balcony and down he went. I turned to listen to the Lord again and low and behold the cat was back being ever so annoying again. I again had to turn around and throw him over the balcony. This went on several times and finally the cat did not return.

I looked over at the Lord and He said, *"I could not have done that for you, you had to do that yourself."*

I learned a good lesson on spiritual authority with this dream and about throwing the old man away, so I could really focus on what the Lord was telling me. Keep in mind that you need to ponder these dreams for them to make sense to you. Try not to make a hasty decision on the interpretation. Remember **all interpretation** comes from the Spirit. God keeps us dependent on Him for interpretation. Even when God speaks we will not understand all of it.

"For My ways are not your ways, My thoughts are not your thoughts, so my ways are higher than your ways."
(Isaiah 55:8)

We are not entitled to an interpretation just because we have the dream. That is just the way it is. Joseph said in Genesis;

"Do not all interpretations belong to God?" (Gen.40:8)

So How Does Interpretation Come?

1. An angel may tell u<u>s</u>.
(Dan7:16) "I came near to one of those who stood there and asked him the truth of all this. So he told me and made me know the interpretation of the thing."
(Dan7:28) "...but I kept the matter of the interpreting angels in my heart and mind."
(This was Gabriel....Gabriel has watch over Israel.)

2. God will speak the dream to us as we dream it. In your mind you will know you are dreaming and you will hear a voice narrating the dream to you.

3. By writing it down. Something happens as we write the dream down, even draw pictures of it, more of the dream will come back to you with understanding.

4. *Journal your way into growth.* Finally last but not least, journal your dreams. If you have a dream in the night and tend to lose them by morning, get up and either write them down or use a recording devise and speak them into it.

5. By writing the dream you understand the dream. God told His prophets to write the visions down.

(1 Chron.28:19)"All this said David, the Lord made me understand in writing with His hand upon me all the details of this pattern."

6. The meaning will become more intense as we mature. In the process

of the search we will find out more than the answer. God loves the search we attempt. It is not unspiritual or immature to search books and scriptures to find the answers. It's the glory of Kings to search. God wants you to become more kingly.

(Prov.25:2) It is the glory of God to conceal a thing, but the glory of Kings is to search out a thing."

Also a few short notes here; if you **dream infrequently** it does not mean you are less spiritual then someone who does seem to dream a lot. Ezekiel had no recorded dreams, Daniel, had visions, **"in my mind on my bed."**
I would offer this, Knock, knock, knock! Ask, ask, and ask! Seek, seek, and seek! The **greater level of peace** I have the more dreams I experience. God says, "Abide in Me."

Remembering Dreams

If you can't remember your dreams it does not mean you are not dreaming or they are unimportant. *"...He seals their instruction"* remember that scripture. Even if you do not recall the dream, if God has something to say, He will seal the instruction by way of the Holy Spirit. You receive the free gift of instruction by God. When you need that information it will "bubble up" out of your well of salvation and be a great blessing to you and others.

When do dreams come to pass?

Dreams may yield immediate fruit or may take months or years to come to pass. (Dan 4:28) Nebuchadnezzar's dream took 12 months to come to pass.

The one I recall the most was I dreamt a huge airplane crashed and people were killed. I saw the American flag was at half mast in mourning. I remember thinking it must have been a huge crash, because the whole country was affected. I was dreaming this simultaneously as it was happening in the natural. I woke and started interceding. My husband turned on the television, the date was 9/11. The Twin Towers in New York City were being destroyed, our country was being attacked, and all those innocent people were dying.

Review of some Interpretation Skills

Keep it simple, don't get fixated on one point, but explore in your dream and you will mature in interpretation. Remember the parable of the mustard seed? If you focused too much on the color, the size, we miss the bigger picture of how it got really big. Dreams are this way also. Look at them in a simple form first. Then use all the little details to add more to the main theme of the dream. Always try to figure the main subject of the dream. Ask yourself, who is this dream about? And what is this dream about?

Remember that the Lord will use other people to represent you also. The Lord will use familiar people to represent ideas to you or concepts He wants to get across to you.

Symbols and Meanings

The following is a short list of symbols that have been very useful to me for interpreting my dreams. I have inserted some words and symbols that are particular to me.

Some of these symbols I acquired from Bob Jones over the last several years as he has helped me interpret my dreams.

Now these symbols have become part of my frame of reference, and they may also become part of yours if you want.

I don't see how anyone could include an entire list of symbolism because it is as infinite as you can dream.

I hope this minor list will begin to let you see how you can develop a spiritual vocabulary list of your own.

Glossary of Symbols

Colors

Amber- The glory of God **(Eze. 1:4: 8:2)**

Blue- The color of the prophetic. The color of
heaven.

Brown-Servant, meekness, humility.

Gold-The color of God's glory. Golden lamp stands. Golden nuggets of wisdom from the "gold mind".

Green-priestly, the color of teaching. A renewal, like spring grass. In someone's hands a gift of teaching. Inexperienced, "He's green

Grey- your grey matter, brain, or your thoughts, not God's. A mixture, not very pure in color. A grey situation, dismal. Lack of color (not of the Lord) Also ashy grey as in death. Ashy horse.(Rev.6:8).

Orange-The sweet companionship of the Lord. Like a sweet orange. "Son Kissed"
Purple- the color of royalty. Royal robes. Red and Blue mixture, = a revelation of the blood. In someone's hands, a gift of intercession.

Red-The Blood of Christ. Passion, love, war, fire, emotions, anger, lust. Red horse. (Rev.6:4) no peace.

Silver-Righteousness (the tongue of the righteous is choice silver) The price of a soul Redemption.(Ex 30:11-16;Rev 21:10)

White-Purity, righteousness, White Horse=Holy Spirit.(Rev.6:2) No blame, innocent.

Rainbow of Colors-God's promises, covenant. A rainbow of God's gifting. Heavenly throne, look at all the colors and record them.

Black- Can be evil, darkness, void. Solomon's Bride was Black. Representing the "Bride" This is the good black isn't it?

Objects

Ashes- Repentance. (Job.42:6)

Atom Bomb-Holy Spirit outpouring. Sign of last days. Miracles Power.

Almond-Fruitfulness (Num 17:8)

Axe-Judgment Also cutting away. ..."every tree that bring not forth good fruit will be hewn down..." (Math. 3:10)
Instrument for work. (Isa 10:15)

Altar- Place of sacrifice(Ex 27:1-8: Rev 6:9)

Anchor- Our security. A place of stability.(Heb 6:19-20)

Banner-Into war. The claiming of an area. Love Banner. Standard to lift up high.(Isa 13:2)

Balm-Healing ministry. (Jer. 8:22)

Bridge -Holy Spirit. The bridge between us and the Son and Father. He speaks only what He hears Jesus speak.

Bed- covenant, rest, salvation, peace and rest. (Ps 41:3)

Bread-Bread of life, sustenance, provision. Christ our food. (John 6:35)

Broom-Sweeping away the old. Cleansing out your house.

Bricks- Works of man, made by man. Imprisonment, bondage. Egypt. Human works For Babel Tower (Gen 11:3)

Banquet Table-Our gifts from God that we may serve others. Provision. Resting and dining on the Lord's goodness.

Brass-Judgment .Disobedience.(Lev 26:19)

Cedar-The tree of royalty. royal tree.(1 Kings 9:11.)

Chair-A place of rest or a place of authority. A position you are in, your occupation or ministry. What kind of chair? A kingly chair, a business man's chair. A position of authority or not.

Clock-Time. The time is now, what time is it? High noon, time for action? Middle of the day or season. Look for applicable numbers.

Closet-your secret place. Your prayer closet. Hidden secrets. (Mt.6:6)

Clothing- covering. Dirty clothes, unrighteous. Dressed in white, righteousness. Dressed in colors, note colors for significance. Coat; mantle or anointing. Protection from the elements. (Mt.5:40)

Cluster of Grapes- Group of believers together. (Isa 65:8)

Cornucopia-Horn of plenty, Abundance, blessed of the Lord. Promise for abundance, filled with fruit? Note what is **in** the cornucopia.

Computer-Your mind. Your analytical self.

Crown-Crown of salvation, kingly power or authority. Glory.

Desert-Barren, dry. Or the place to hear the Father's voice, Jesus did this to hear His Father's voice, went into the desert. A Spiritual dry place also. Note circumstances, and your other surroundings in the dream.

Door- New opportunity in Christ or from Him. "I am the door of the sheep (John 10:2, 7,9). An entrance, an invitation. A way to get there.

Drugs-Addiction to something. Influence, witchcraft. Medicine and healing.

Earthquake-disaster, natural or spiritual upheaval. Judgment. (Isaiah 29;6.)

Eating-Fellowship, covenant, provision. Partaking with the Lord.... (He that eateth with me... (John 13:18)

Egg-That which life comes from. A beginning. Potential is there for new birth.

Electricity-Power, Holy Spirit power. Lightening bolts are similar to this.

Falling-losing control, no support. Financial, or moral. Falling away from the things of God.

Feathers-Covering, Spirit. "He shall cover you with His feathers..."(Psalm 91;4). Sealing of the Holy Spirit.

Fountain-Fountain of Life, understanding. Fountain of Living waters,(Jer2;13) The Holy Spirit. Three tiered fountain, Trinity.

Fence- Boundaries in the Spirit or natural. Religious doctrines, traditions. Breaking down the fences or boundaries, or are you building up the defenses or fortresses.

Footstool-"Thine enemies as your footstool"(Psalm 110:1) Stepping up and using something as your footstool. A place to rest your feet, on your walk.

Fire-The Word in your mouth, passion, heat, intense, burning away the old. The passion of the Lord, His Glory on the Throne, "Is not my Word like a fire?"(Jer.23:29) Flames of Fire, Holy Spirit. Heavenly visitation.

Fishing-Evangelizing. "fishers of men" (Math.4; 19). Fish=humanity.

Flooding-Drenched in the Spirit. Or, drowned in sin, or judgment, temptation, etc.

Flowers-Opening up. Glory. A sign of a new thing. Before the seed comes the flower. Temporary.
 "I am the Rose of Sharon, the Lilly of the Valley."

Food-Foundational truth from the Word of God. The meat and the milk. Provision.

Forrest- Thick and dense, darkness and confusion. Sometimes a place of protection, A forest of Cedars with covering for example. I Can't see the forest for the trees. Think again about context of the dream.

Fog- Confusion, can't "see" clearly. I'm in a fog. Clouded thoughts. Clouded issues for decision making.

Fortress-Salvation, The Rock of...That which protects you and keeps the enemy out. (Ps 61:3)

Gardening-Field of pleasant labor, in ministry. Bringing up the little seedlings. Plowing new ground.

Garden=church or field of labor. Your heart.

Hair- Covering..."her hair is given her as a covering."(1 Corinth.11: 15).

Highway-The way to get there. The truth, the way of life. Road splits= decision time, the narrow path. The way of Holiness...

(Isaiah 35; 8) <u>Dead End</u>, time to look again, stop where you are, turn around take the better road.

Horns- Authority, power, Anointing, righteous. (..".But the horns of the righteous shall be exalted" (Psalms 75:10)

Honey- Sweetness. Strength. Power by the Holy Spirit. God experience. The Lord sees you as sweet unto Him.

House-House of the Lord. That which you are comfortable in, you have made this house your home where you reside."And we are His house" if we hold onto our courage. (Heb. 3:6.)

Halo-Around someone's head or and aura. God's glory about them. ("The Son is the radiance of God's glory." (Heb. 1:3)

Key-The key, the wisdom the knowledge of it. God's hand in it. The most important factor, "the key to it." Opening new doors with the key, an invitation. Key of David, Kingdom Power; Key of Hades; authority of spirit realm.
(Isa 22:22)(Rev 1:18)

Kiss- A covenant. A covenant breaker(Judas). Seduction. Deception. Lust.
Holy Kiss as greeting.

Knives-Sharp truth, or anger with words. Revelation. Cut it away. Stab in the back.

Ladder-Where you go up or come down. Open Heaven. Jacob's ladder. Son of Man connecting Heaven to earth. (Gen 28:12:John 1:51)

Leaves-healing for the nations. Covering yourself with fig leaves, temporary hiding from the Lord, as in Adam and Eve. Falling leaves, a late season, as in the autumn.

Map-The direction, note direction. Which way Lord? Note cities or particular places on the map.

Money- Natural or spiritual provision. The trusting of man's power over God's power.

Newspaper-Important current up to date announcement, good or bad.

Darkness and all that is associated with the darkness, sin and ignorance, without 'Light"

Oil-Anointing, healing. That which greases the move of the Spirit. Oil in your automobile. Oil that moves your ministry.

Pots or Pans-Vessels, God's vessel's ready to be filled, clay pots.

Rain-The move of the Spirit. Revival of the Spirit. A drought. No blessings.

River-River of the Spirit, where the spirit flows, cleansing, rivers of living waters.(John 7:37-39)

Roof-Covering. What is the roof made from? The mind of man.

Running-Running away or towards. Strife, anxiety to hurry. "So run, that ye may obtain."(1 Corinth.924.)

Seed-Word of God. That which you plant expecting good fruit. Seed that is good or bad, out of the abundance of your heart produces it. A new beginning. A new harvest, a new work, the essence of it.

What it takes to make it grow. Faith, abundance or lack of it. The grain of a mustard seed.

Sword- Word of the Spirit. That which is the Lord's to cut away or edify. Two edged sword.

Smoke-His Glory, His manifest presence. The saint's prayers as incense. Sodom and Gomorrah..."and lo the smoke of the country went up as the smoke of a furnace."(Gen.19;28) God's judgment is manifest in smoke.

Sun-Jesus, the Light of the World. The protection, the heat."*For the Lord God is a sun and a shield."(Psalm 84:11)*.

Swimming-operating in the gifts of the Spirit. Prophesying.

Swimming Pool-Your spiritual place or your spiritual condition. Good or bad. Healing Pools of Bethesda. A place of healing.

Tea-Good news, refreshment from the Lord. Stimuli from the Lord to move.

Teaching, Sweet teaching. " Tea time," rest of the Lord.

Tears-Sorrow, repentance. Tears of Joy. Cleansing the soul.

Thorns-Distraction, or hindrance or reminders. Persecution. Miner fuss or disturbance.

Trees- Genealogy, curses or blessings. Family trees. " *All the trees of the field shall know that I have brought down the high tree and have exalted the low tree."(Ezekiel 17;24)* Trees of righteousness. A shelter. Note the different types of tree and color of leaves, what season etc. for further interpretation. We are the tree.

Trumpet-The clear trumpet, the clear voice , the true prophet. The clear warning. What color is the trumpet?

Wind-He will make His angels winds. Winds of change. Spirit Winds. The Holy Spirit

Doctrine, *"Be not children tossed to and fro by the winds of doctrine..."(Eph.* 4;14) Religious spirit. Law.

Window-Revelation. Seeing into the Spirit. Truth. Prophesy. A way into for blessing. Shedding light on the darkness, open the window. Fresh air, the Spirit moves in.

Numbers

One-Unity, Primary. God. The beginning, In the beginning God. Source

Two-Two witnesses. Testimony.

Three-divine completeness, Number of the God Head. Perfect testimony.

Four-. Four winds, creation, four seasons.

Five-grace, atonement, life, the cross, fivefold ministries.

Six-number man, man was created on the 6th day. Beast, Satan.

Seven-spiritual perfection. And completeness.

Eight-number of new beginnings, resurrection, and regeneration. The beginning of a new age an order.

Nine-The completeness or conclusion of a matter. The fullness. Number of the Holy Spirit. Number for Fruit of the womb.

Ten-number of law, order, government, restoration, antichrist kingdom.

Twelve-Divine Government
Thirteen-Rebellion, *"and in the thirteenth year they rebelled."* (Gen.14;4)

Fourteen-Number of Passover

Twenty-four-Heavenly government.

Thirty-Number of Maturity and consecration to ministry.

Forty-judgment

Fifty-jubilee, liberty, freedom.

Seventy-Number prior to increase, a multitude.

<u>Animals</u>

Bears-White Bear=death to self, righteousness. **Black Bear**=fear of man. **Brown bear**= fear of the Lord. Cursing as in the destroyer bears of Elisha.

Bees- curses, chastisement, stings of hurt and pain by ones words or actions. Too busy, or "busy as a bee." Produces sweetness.

Butterfly- Change, freedom, metamorphosis.

Birds-confusion, wrong message. Evil Spirits

Dove-The Holy Spirit Dove

Dog-contention, unclean spirits, note how dog's attitude is, friendly, mean. Unbelievers, evil workers. Lack of faith. Aggressive, etc. Note color of the dog, also.

Mice-or rats, thoughts and works of the mind. Unclean things.

Monkeys-Mischief. "Monkey on my back."

Owls-Wisdom, white owls, pure wisdom from God. Birds evil spirits.

Horses-represent the "flesh".
White Horse, "Holy Spirit." Strength, swiftness, spiritual support. Power

Mountain Lion-Unavoidable problems

Lion Lion of Judah, Kingship, royalty. Strength, boldness of courage good and evil

Body Parts

Hands- Service, ministry. Worship.(Ps 134:2)

Right Hand-Faith, blessing, yet to come.

Left Hand-ministry, this moment, judgment.

Hip or Thigh-commitment

Fingers-Thumb=Apostolic, government. Pointer=Prophet, guide.   Middle evangelist, gatherer. Fourth finger,=Teacher, grounder. Small finger=Pastor, guard.

Eyes-eyes to see. Sight, insight, vision.

Ears-ears to hear. Channel to receive faith. Mt 13:9,15,16,43)

Heel-crushing power, Victory(Gen 3:15)

Knees-Worship, adoration. Intercession.

Feet- Walking out your ministry. Bowing at His feet. Complete submission to Lord.

Kidney-(reins) inner drives and motives of the heart.

Bosom- Place of Love affection intimacy. (Luke. 16:22)

Breath-Impartation of Life (Gen 2:7)

SUMMARY

This book is merely meant to stimulate you to further engage in the ideas and thoughts that God is forever speaking in ways we may miss if not stimulated to them.

I am not an expert in this but my heart is to help in any way I can.
I do not have the academic credentials to be an expert. Without the help of the Holy Spirit none of this book would be possible.
Hopefully the information I have provided will be in some way useful to you in your quest to hear God.
If I have given you the desire to seek God in this subject matter, then I believe it has fulfilled the purpose I intended it to.
May you be blessed with every good thing from above.
Yours faithfully in Christ,
Brenda McDonald

"Redeeming Power"
Original art by Brenda McDonald

Made in the USA
Charleston, SC
21 January 2012